5/00

The Life and Work of...

Mary Cassatt

Ernestine Giesecke

Heinemann Library
Des Plaines, Illinois

©2000 Reed Educational & Professional Publishing
Published by Heinemann Library,
an imprint of Reed Educational & Professional Publishing,
1350 East Touhy Avenue, Suite 240 West
Des Plaines, IL 60018

Customer Service 1-888-454-2279

Text designed by Sandy Newell
Printed in Hong Kong/China

04 03 02 01 00
10 9 8 7 6 5 4 3 2 1

Library of Congress Cataloging-in-Publication Data
Giesecke, Ernestine, 1945-
     Mary Cassatt / Ernestine Giesecke.
        p. cm. -- (The life and work of–) (Heinemann profiles)
     Includes bibliographical references and index.
     Summary: Introduces the life and work of Mary Cassatt, discussing her early years, life in the United States and Paris, and development as an artist.
        ISBN 1-57572-955-5 (lib. bdg.)
     1. Cassatt, Mary, 1844-1926 Juvenile literature. 2. Artists-
-United States Biography Juvenile literature. [1. Cassatt, Mary,
1844-1926. 2. Artists 3. Women Biography. 4. Painting, American.
5. Art appreciation] I. Title. II. Series. III. Series:
Heinemann profiles.
N6537.C35G54   1999
759. 13—dc21   99-14557
[B]   CIP

Acknowledgments
The Publisher would like to thank the following for permission to reproduce photographs:

The Pennsylvania Academy of Fine Arts, Philadelphia, pp. 4, 8; The Denver Art Museum, Anonymous Bequest, p. 5; Drawing of Cassatt Family, Peter Baumgartner, 1854, Anonymous Owner, p. 6; Fine Arts Museums of San Francisco, Museum purchase, William H. Nobel Bequest Fund, 1979.35, p. 7; Founders Society Purchase, Robert H. Tannahill Foundation Fund, The Detroit Institute of Arts, p. 9; Corbis/Bettmann, p. 10; The Roland P. Murdock Collection, Wichita Art Museum, Wichita, Kansas, p.11; Bibliotheque Nationale, Department des Estampes, p. 12; Philadelphia Museum of Art, W.P. Wilstach Collection, p. 13; Erich Lessing/Art Resource, p. 14; Sterling and Francine Clark Art Institute, p. 15; The Bridgeman Art Library International, Ltd., pp. 16, 23; Collection of Mr. and Mrs. Paul Mellon, ©1999 Board of Trustees, National Gallery of Art, Washington, 1878, p.17; National Portrait Gallery, Smithsonian Institution. Gift of the Morris and Gwendolyn Cafritz Foundation and the Regents' Major Acquisitions fund, Smithsonian Institution, p. 18; The Metropolitan Museum of Art, Bequest of Edith H. Proskauer, 1975, p. 19; Anonymous Gift in Honor of Eugenia Cassatt Madeira courtesy, Museum of Fine Arts, Boston, p. 20; M. Theresa B. Hopkins Fund courtesy, Museum of Fine Arts, Boston, p. 21; Photograph ©Bibliotheque Nationale de France, Paris, p. 22; Anonymous Owner, p. 24; Los Angeles County Museum of Art, gift of Mrs. Fred Hathaway Bixby Bequest, p. 25; Lee B. Ewing/F.A. Sweet Papers, Archives of American Art, Smithsonian Institution, p. 26; photograph courtesy of Terra Museum of American Art, Chicago, p. 27.

Cover photo: *Five O'Clock Tea,* Mary Cassatt/M. Theresa B. Hopkins Fund courtesy, Museum of Fine Arts, Boston

Some words in this book are in bold, **like this.** You can find out what they mean by looking in the Glossary.

Contents

Who Was Mary Cassatt?

Mary Cassatt was an American artist. She was a successful woman painter at a time when most painters were men.

Most of Mary's art shows **scenes** from everyday life. Some of her most well-known paintings are of mothers and children.

Early Years

Mary was born May 22, 1844. She grew up in Philadelphia, Pennsylvania. When Mary was a young child, her family moved to Germany. She was ten years old when this picture was made. Later, Mary's family moved to France.

In school, Mary studied many subjects. She studied drawing and music. When Mary became an artist, she painted **portraits** of her family. This portrait shows her mother, Katherine Cassatt.

Philadelphia Art Student

When Mary was a teenager, her family moved back to Philadelphia. Mary was 17 years old when she went to the Pennsylvania Academy of Fine Arts. Mary is the girl on the right.

Mary learned to draw from life and by studying other works of art. She liked to ride horses with her older brother, Alexander. This is a **portrait** Mary made of him when she was older.

Paris Art Student

When Mary was 21 years old, she traveled to Paris. She wanted to study art. Like other students, she studied works of art by the **old masters.** She copied paintings in the **Louvre.**

Mary studied **Madonna and Child** paintings.
Her studies helped her to paint **contemporary**
mothers caring for their small children.

The Salon

In 1868, when Mary was 24 years old, her work was chosen to be shown in the **Salon** in Paris. The Salon was a place where artists who made excellent paintings showed their work. Mary wrote her parents that being chosen would help her become well-known.

This painting is called *On the Balcony during Carnival*. It is like many of the paintings Mary made when she first moved to Paris. It is the kind of painting the Salon judges liked.

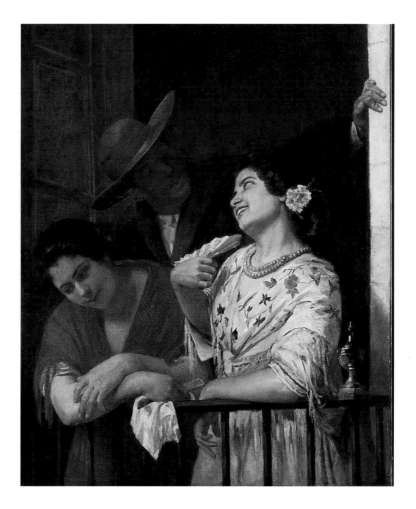

Professional Artist

Mary **exhibited** in the **Salon** for a few more years. She grew tired of having to paint what would please the judges at the Salon.

Mary did not want to paint **models** anymore.
She did not want to use dark colors. She
wanted to paint things as she saw them.

Changing Her Way

In 1877, Mary met Edgar Degas. Edgar introduced Mary to other painters. These painters were known as the **Impressionists**. The Impressionists painted **scenes** of everyday life.

The Impressionists painted with **splotches** of color. Mary liked the colors they used and the way they used them. She made this painting soon after she met Edgar Degas.

Joining the Impressionists

Mary and Edgar became friends for life. They visited each other's **studios**. They talked about their work. They gave each other ideas. Edgar Degas painted this **portrait** of Mary.

18

Mary liked many of the **Impressionists'** ideas. She used their ideas to make paintings she liked. She began to use lighter colors and paint more freely.

Painting Real Life

Most **Impressionists** painted outdoor **scenes**. Mary used the Impressionist ideas, but she painted indoor scenes and things from everyday life. The paintings tell us about Mary's life.

Most of Mary's paintings are **portraits** of her family, friends, and neighbors. Many things in Mary's paintings belonged to her. Look at the silver tea set on page 20. You can see it in the painting on this page.

Painting Women

Mary lived in a lively part of Paris near this **café**. Painters, musicians, and writers met at cafés to talk about their ideas. Mary and the women she knew read newspapers. They wanted to keep up with the **current events**.

Mary sometimes painted women reading the newspaper. This was something new in painting. At that time, most artists painted **models** who **posed** just for the painting.

Mothers and Children

Mary never married or had any children. Mary's brother, Alexander, and his family stayed with her when they visited Europe. Mary loved her nieces and nephews. She often painted pictures of them.

Mary spent hours on each drawing and painting. Yet many of her drawings and paintings show just one second in time. This child looks happy and safe in her mother's arms.

French Countryside

Mary bought a home near Paris. She spent most of her time there. Her **studio** was on the first floor of her home. She could look out onto her gardens and a pond.

26

This picture of ducks was **inspired** by the pond behind Mary's home. This picture is a **print**. A print allows an artist to make many copies of the same picture. Mary worked hard and became very good at making prints.

A Lasting Impression

During the last years of Mary's life, her eyesight failed. She could not paint. Mary Cassatt died June 14, 1926. She was 82 years old.

Today, people are still amazed at the feelings of closeness and love that they have when they look at a picture by Mary Cassatt.

Timeline

1844	Mary Cassatt born, May 22
1861	Mary begins her studies at Pennsylvania Academy of Fine Arts
1861–65	U. S. Civil War
1865–70	Mary travels in Europe
1868	Mary's work first **exhibited** (the Salon)
1879	Mary exhibits with the **Impressionists**
1893	First individual exhibition
1900	World's Fair in Paris, France
1914–18	World War I
	Mary moves to Italy to avoid the war
1920	Women in the U.S. win the right to vote
1926	Mary Cassatt dies, June 14

Glossary

café place that serves food or coffee

contemporary living at the same time

current event something happening at the present time

exhibit to show art work in public

Impressionists group of artists who painted outside to make colorful pictures

inspire to influence or guide

Louvre museum in Paris, France

Madonna and Child work of art that shows Mary and baby Jesus

model person an artist paints or draws

old master famous artist with great skill

portrait painting, drawing, or photograph of a person

pose to sit or stand still for an artist

print one of many copies

Salon place in Paris where artists were invited to show their artwork

scene place where something happens

splotch large spot

studio place where an artist works

Index

More Books to Read

Baxter, Nicola. *Amazing Colors.* Minneapolis, Minn.: Children's Press, 1995.

Conlon, Laura. *Painters.* Vero Beach, Fla.: Rourke Press, Incorporated, 1994.

Venezia, Mike. *Mary Cassatt.* Minneapolis, Minn.: Children's Press, 1990.

More Artwork to See

The Letter. 1890-91. National Gallery of Art, Washington, D.C., and The Chicago Art Institute, Chicago, Ill.

Sleepy Baby. 1910. Dallas Museum of Fine Art, Dallas, Tex.

Girl Brushing Her Hair. 1886. National Gallery of Art, Washington, D.C.

The Lady at the Tea Table. 1883. Metropolitan Museum of Art, New York, N.Y.